Plain Fat C
Seeks Guy who
Likes Broccoli

Humorous Personal Ads
Written by Real People

Collected
by
Kathy Hinckley

Cartoons
by
Peter Hesse

GIBBS · SMITH
→P
PUBLISHER
SALT LAKE CITY

First Edition
99 98 97   10 9 8 7 6 5 4 3 2 1

This is a Peregrine Smith Book, published by
Gibbs Smith, Publisher
P.O. Box 667
Layton, Utah 84041

Design by Peter Hesse
Printed and bound in the U.S.A.

Library of Congress Cataloging-in-Publication Data
Plain fat chick seeks guy who likes broccoli-- / collected by Kathy
   Hinckley ; cartoons by Peter Hesse.
       p.   cm.
     "A Peregrine Smith book."
     ISBN 0-87905-810-2
     1. Personals--Miscellanea. 2. Dating (Social customs)-
   -Miscellanea. I. Hinckley, Kathleen W., 1948– .
   HQ801.P6 1997
   646.77--dc21   96-39227
                                                       CIP

Reality and Fantasy

"Plain Fat Chick Seeks Guy Who Likes Broccoli." The personal ad jumped off the page at me. I was impressed! Plain Fat Chick could look into her mirror and use the F-A-T word with confidence and humor. I clipped the ad and started my collection.

I was hooked. A new Kathy was born: the Collector of Truth in the personal ads of America. I saved ads that made me giggle. Candid ads. Bizarre ads. But — above all — honest ads, such as the man who prefers women with unshaven legs, a woman with a jelly belly, and a cowboy who admits to being uglier than a bucket of rattlesnakes.

Most of us are not beauty queens or Olympic champs. In reality, we have warts, tattoos, beer bellies, gray hair, and double chins. Our thighs look like road maps and our rose-colored glasses will too soon be swapped for bifocals.

We hope you enjoy the reality and the fantasy in these ads.

Acknowledgements

Thank you to my family for believing in me, for without their support, my idea may not have become a reality.

My friends listed below helped too! They collected personals, brainstormed with me, and contributed in numerous other ways.

Jerry Anderson	Jan Malmberg
Marta Berube	Elizabeth Mills
Sharon Boatwright	Eileen Polakoff
Bob Christopher	Gordon Remington
Pat Hatcher	Vicki Watson
James Jeffrey	Patti Zangari

A special thanks to Liz Hesse for editorial assistance.

Contents

Key to Abbreviations

A	ASIAN	H	HISPANIC	ND	NON-DRINKER
B	BLACK	ISO	IN SEARCH OF	NS	NON-SMOKER
C	CHRISTIAN	L	LATINO OR LESBIAN	P	PROFESSIONAL
D	DIVORCED	J	JEWISH	S	SINGLE
F	FEMALE	LTR	LONG-TERM RELATIONSHIP	W	WHITE
G	GAY	M	MALE OR MARRIED	WW	WIDOWED

Example: **SWM** = SINGLE WHITE MALE;   **S/DBF** = SINGLE/DIVORCED BLACK FEMALE

GOLD DIGGERS

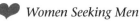 *Women Seeking Men*

BUXOM BLONDE

Me: buxom blonde with blue eyes. You: elderly, marriage-minded millionaire with bad heart.

Women Seeking Men

I HATE MY JOB

If you marry me, I can quit. Over-educated, left-leaning, politically active SWF, 40, seeks SWM. Likes dining out. No one's ever asked me to put a bag over my head. How about you?

 Women Seeking Men

CHAMPAGNE IS PREFERRED

Looking for some fabulous arm ornament to escort me around town. I enjoy a witty man with a good finance background. Champagne is preferred. A tall man is a plus, active and physically fit, non-smoker. Age 35-45 preferred. Let's share a good friendship.

 Women Seeking Men

I'M A MATERIALISTIC FEMALE

I'll be the best looking blind date you ever had. I am funny, sexy, and angelic. The catch: I am broke, head-strong, very sassy, a materialistic female with high hopes that a mogul-CEO will be smitten with me.

 Women Seeking Men

SEEK NEUROSURGEON WITH NICE CAR

Woman from Guadalajara seeks financially secure neurosurgeon. Preferably with very nice car. Find me behind a cash register temporarily, honest!

 *Men Seeking Women*

BECOME MY WIDOW

Bring joy into my life, then become my widow with a minimum lifetime pension of $1,500 per month, plus other benefits. Call or write.

 *Men Seeking Women*

YOU HAVE EVERYTHING THAT MONEY CAN BUY

except that special person who isn't for sale at stores. Who can give you hugs, kisses, and TLC. Who is trustworthy, European-born male, attractive, non-smoker, 30s, 5'7", blue eyes, in good shape. For fun and more. If not satisfied you'll get your money back!

TALK SHOW STARS

 *Men Seeking Women*

BIG TOOTSIES

Big female with big feet sought by SWM 6'3", 210 lbs., who loves giving TLC to big tootsies. Age 18-80.

Men Seeking Women

I LOVE UNSHAVEN LEGS

BM, 40s, professional, drug and disease free, seeks a most serious female 24-40, drug and disease free, with hairy legs to spend quality fun time together. Love traveling, personal computing, music, movies, much more. You — kind, energetic, full of life, positive-minded, and communicative. If you like a kind, very sensitive, caring and gentle male, and if material things are not the focus on life, then please get in touch.

 *Men Seeking Women*

THERE AIN'T MANY OF US

Sensitive, sexy, unconventional vegetarian male, 45, seeks female homesteading partner. Staunch environmentalist planning to live without car or electricity. Sound like the good life to you too? Please write! There ain't many of us.

 Men Seeking Women

WORLD-FAMOUS PLASTIC SURGEON

seeks three ladies to travel with.

 *Men Seeking Women*

CD GIRLFRIEND

Before you read any further, CD means cross-dresser. That's what I enjoy. I would love to have a girlfriend that would like to go out with me...and wouldn't get jealous if I got more wolf whistles. I'd also make an excellent boyfriend, no matter what I'm wearing.

 *Men Seeking Women*

BALD BEAUTIES

Attractive, white, Christian male, 30, 6', 250 lbs. seeking bald or balding women who need their special beauty appreciated. Interested in both romantic, platonic relationships.

 *Men Seeking Women*

RU ILLUSTRATED

If you can't leave home without body art, darling, I should be your counterpart. Caring SWM, sharply designed for sharing, requires female tattooey and piercey for an intimate start.

OLD FARTS & HOT GRANDMAS

 *Men Seeking Women*

TARZAN LONELY IN JUNGLE, NEED FAT OLD JANE

WM, 67, 6'3", 204 lbs., Tarzan lonely in jungle, need fat old Jane 68 to 99 years old. Like 'em movies, eat in and out of jungle. When Tarzan ship come in, he at airport. Like swing in Las Vegas, swing on beach, but don't like sand. No smoke in jungle. Love wrinkles and white hair. No like 'em skinny Jane. Quick, send up smoke signal. Start off fun.

Women Seeking Men

MY CAT DIED

last week. He weighed 23 lbs., slept on my bed and was xenophobic. You see the problem. So, if you're male, pushing 60 or past, smart, fit, funny, write. Soon. I could start browsing at Save-A-Stray any second!

 Men Seeking Women

OLD DUFFER HAS FIRE IN FURNACE

WM, 60, 6'3", 215 lbs., non-smoker, non-drinker, "old duffer" with hair that'll keep ya smiling. Seeks non-smoking, weight near proportionate, hedonist WF accomplice with a little fire in furnace.

 Women Seeking Men

SEEK MAN WITH ORIGINAL TEETH (NO DENTURES)

Wholesome whole-hearted, homeowner, nice looking WF, 63, 5'3", 115 lbs. Enjoys soothing music, gracious living, caresses, smiles, conversation, beach/nature walks, movies, dancing, togetherness, with caring, intelligent man. No dentures; chemistry, a must.

 Women Seeking Men

GOOD DRIVING RECORD?

Widowed white female, 77, would like to meet caring gentleman, 70-80, for companion to move in and share expenses. Must be non-smoker, non-drinker, and have good driving record.

 Men Seeking Women

NAUGHTY LADY OK

Wonderful gentleman, dark-haired, caring, home loving, exciting, sexy, cologned grandpa seeks 5' heavyset, chubby, slender, smiling, home cooking WWF retiree 57-68-79 grandmom for fun cuddling, day trips, swimming, music, malls, TV, easy relationship. Mischievous, naughty, kind lady OK.

 Women Seeking Men

DISLIKE SHOES AND HOUSEWORK

Lady, 63, 5'7", 135 lbs. of fun, smoker, social drinker, a lover not a fighter, like dancing, gardening togetherness. Dislike dishonesty, shoes and housework.

Men Seeking Women

FAITHFUL TO THE END

Retired 63 yr. old, twice a widower due to cancer. Known only two women intimately in my life & loved & married both of them. I'm 5'10", 170 lbs., and in excellent health. Light snow on the roof, but fire still roars in the basement. I maintain clean house, owned and run by a 12-yr.-old cat. Bath and refrigerator clean and nothing grows in either. Completely potty trained and nobody picks up after me. Do all laundry by whites & color, bleach & non-bleach. Avid square dancer, walks, long drives, exploring back roads, romantic candle dinners with wine, good music & good movies. Light smoker trying to quit. In search of another one of God's petite finest for next 20 years or more. Must be very physical, hugs, holding hands, touching & whatever comes natur- ally, & being told how important and lovely she is to me.

 Men Seeking Women

OLD SAILOR

I am an old sailor (90) looking for a 30- to 40-year-old slim, physically fit attractive lady to do a circumnaviga- tion with. Do not respond unless you fit the above parameters.

 Women Seeking Men

PANTS MUST FIT THE HINEY

Healthy, active, young 74, DWF, look and act 60, 5'3", 140 lbs., non- smoker, you may, social drinker, many interests — dancing, travel, fishing, boating, camping, also quiet times. Need good male counterpart, 60-75, to share life and what's over the next hill. Am a Wrangler butt person, so pants have to fit the hiney!! I'm more into jeans and slacks than lace and pearls. Have good sense of humor, easy going, compatible. Would relocate.

 Men Seeking Women

A LITTLE ARTHRITIS

Lonely DWM, 71 yrs., 5'8", 205 lbs., blondish/grey eyes, a little bald, wear glasses, pretty good health for my age. A little arthritis. Good personality, easy to get along with. Own my own remodeled home. I drive. Seeking SWF, 60s, about the same height, weight to 240 lbs., (I love large women — when you catch hold of them you have something — the skinny ones ask how much money you have).

Men Seeking Women

STILL HAVE TESTOSTERONE

Very funny man, 60 yrs., 5'7", 210 lbs., looking for smart, funny gal to share time with. I still have some hair, teeth, and testosterone left. Come and get me.

 Women Seeking Men

I NEED A YOUNG MAN TO DRIVE AWAY MY MIDDLE-AGE BLUES

To paraphrase the uppity blues women: Men my age are all married, boring, or tired. I gotta find a young man cuz I want to feel desired. Don't worry about what people say; age ain't nothing but a number. Like a rare wine, we don't get older, we get better. Help in the garden, take me out on the town. Pleasing you will be my priority.

 Men Seeking Women

SMOKES, DRINKS, PLAYS HORSES

Total reprobate, late 50s, smokes, drinks, plays horses. Produce motion pictures and television. Believe that laughter is the best aphrodisiac. Seeking pleasant, honest, happy lady, 45+. Young stuff forget it.

 Women Seeking Men

HOT FLASHES

SWF, just turned 50 and looking forward to the excitement of adolescence. Immaturity keeps me young and Miss Clairol keeps me red-headed.

 *Men Seeking Women*

TIME AND MONEY ON MY HANDS

Looking for lovely sensual woman to enjoy hot spa and heated pool in my home, travel to Vegas, Hawaii, and Florida. Must have long hair, wear lipstick. Loving sports a plus. I'm 60, widowed with time and money on my hands.

 *Women Seeking Men*

BRING READING LIST & AN EKG

The 60s are better in retrospect. If your brain cells activate before your hormones, and you're over 40, call me. Late 40s woman, friend to men, ready to come out of retirement. Come with a reading list and an EKG. I'll be the one in the jeans and bifocals.

 Men Seeking Women

MY OWN WEIGHT CHART

Why would I expect to meet the woman of my dreams, when I get lines like these? "I am weight proportionate," she sez. Turns out to be 5'2", 195 lbs. "I could lose maybe 10 lbs.," she sez. Turns out to be 5'5", 186, and I am getting sick over dinner. Time for Tums. Read my idea of what I consider "proportionate." I am an honest, successful, witty, playful, good looking and creative 38-year-old man. Do you exist? Do you fit the bill?

5'2" > 103-110	5'4" > 108-117	5'6" > 115-126
5'3" > 105-113	5'5" > 110-120	5'7" > 120-130

Men Seeking Women

NICE HAIR AND FEET REQUIRED

SPBM, 32, educated, very focused, settled and family oriented. ISO intelligent, classy SBF, under 35 and 130 lbs. Must have nice hair and feet. One child okay, but not two. Seeking long-term relationship and marriage.

 Women Seeking Men

DO YOU QUALIFY?

Don't call if you are uneducated; unemployed, unhealthy smoker, alcoholic, drug user; felon, under 30 years old, 5'10", 170 lbs.; over 40 years old, 6'8", 230 lbs; like cats, channel surfing; make less than $30,000 annually; or have body parts pierced. Others feel free.

 Men Seeking Women

MUST NOT BE PREGNANT

SWM ISO SWF. Must be honest, nice, neat, slim, trim and not pregnant. Must have a good disposition with all the buck, kick and fidget out. Must enjoy me, country life, rodeos, 2 step, and appreciate nice things. Can you make my team?

 Women Seeking Men

NO CREATIVE COMBERS

Slender, pretty, DWF, 50, seeks attractive DWM, 45-55, to share fun, travel, quality home time. No smokers, drinkers, pot bellies or creative combers. Must be secure, blue-collared, comfortable in jeans and like country music.

 *Men Seeking Women*

BE EMPLOYED, CHILDLESS, AND AVAILABLE DURING THE DAY

SBM, 5'10", 45, 200 lbs., wants employed, childless, non-smoking female who is available during the day (I work 4 pm to midnight). Prefer 200-300 lbs., 28-58 years old, over 5'5". Within a 20-mile radius of Yankee Stadium.

Men Seeking Women

5'4 1/2" TO 5'6 1/2" ONLY

SWM, 42, 5'8", 155 lbs., 9.8% body fat, training for professional tennis. Seeking girlfriend, 5'4 1/2" to 5'6 1/2", long hair, aerobically fit, generously balanced figure, age 25-29, no kids, non-smoker, and I'll appreciate it every day.

TRUE CONFESSIONS

 *Men Seeking Women*

PERFECT MATE WANTED

Love-starved SWM seeking a trophy wife with upper-class looks and attitude to take to my next high school reunion. I am 36 and have never had a girlfriend.

Men Seeking Women

GAY WIFE WANTED

Good-looking, successful attorney, 29, 100-percent closeted and healthy, gay Jewish male, seeks feminine, closeted gay wife.

 Women Seeking Men

I'M PREGNANT

SWF, 21, 5', ISO SWM, 21-30, who wants to settle down. Must like kids, and be willing to get involved with pregnant woman and be financially secure.

 Men Seeking Women

CAN YOU LOOK BEYOND MY CHAIR?

SWM, 49, 6', slender build. I'm a little shy but very caring, honest, persistent, NS, ND. Twenty-five years ago I became paraplegic from a spinal cord injury. I would like to meet someone who can accept that I am partially paralyzed and see me for who I am, a man. I have endless love for the right woman and am not looking for a nursemaid. I enjoy computers, the outdoors and, of course, children. Can you look beyond my chair?

 Men Seeking Women

FLATULENT REDNECK

Fat, flatulent, over 40, cigar-smoking redneck seeks sexy woman with big hair to cook, clean, and pick up unemployment checks.

 Men Seeking Women

BEER GUZZLER

I drink a lot of beer, smoke a lot of cigars, and watch football nonstop from September to January. I seek a woman, 18-32, to share this with.

 Women Seeking Men

I DON'T COOK OR DO WINDOWS

DWF, brown hair, brown eyes, 63, 5', 100 lbs., lazy procrastinator, don't cook, don't do windows. Not a glamour gal. Love the outdoors, my German Shepherd, football, travel, gardening, Europe, cruises, dining out, flying single-engine airplanes, Chopin, Beethoven, Gershwin, Sinatra. Interests too numerous to list. Don't like facial hair, blue jeans, foul language. Looking for a friend similar interests, patient, understanding, caring, honest. I smoke.

Women Seeking Men

ALLERGIC TO CATS ...

not horses, pickups or steak. SWF, attorney, 31, thin, seeks straightforward M, 5'11"+, 28-40, no baggage, with horse trailer.

 Men Seeking Women

SEEK FLOOZY SIDEKICK

Professional Gambler and Card Counter seeks floozy sidekick for Vegas trip; all expenses paid. Are you 21-29, beautiful and adventurous enough to play my game? If so, call me, because the jewel in the desert beckons.

Men Seeking Women

ON TRACK
TO BECOME
A PRIEST

until 2 months ago, when I realized spiritual love wasn't enough. Please help ease me into the physical world. Be sincere.

 Men Seeking Men

GAY GUY

44, handsome, mustache, seeks fat, husky cigar smoker.

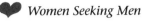 *Women Seeking Men*

HARD UP
& DESPERATE

SWF, 39, looks older and fatter. Mean, bossy, possibly schizophrenic. Hates skiing, hiking, camping, music and long walks. Loves Las Vegas, Scotch, intelligence. Actually very pretty (if you can get past the double chins), educated and nuts. Call if you smoke.

 *Men Seeking Women*

I'M NOT A LEPER

I'm just herpes positive, SBM, 39 years young, 5'11", 160 lbs., workaholic. ISO SF, for friendship and LTR.

Men Seeking Women

I LIKE LOUD MUSIC

SM, 18 yrs., smoker. My favorite food is pizza. I treat a woman with respect. I enjoy parties, bike riding, and having fun. I am currently seeking employment. I'm looking for a woman with long dark hair and dark brown eyes. An open-minded woman with a sense of humor, who is 5'1", 95 lbs. & 18-21 yrs.

Men Seeking Women

I LIVE WITH THREE ANIMALS

WM, 50, but looks 49¼, seeks a person who is 1) female, 2) breathing, and 3) nice. I enjoy movies, dining, dancing, outdoors, and watching TV. I live with three animals: my dog, my cat, and my brother. I'm a nice guy who enjoys people.

 Men Seeking Women

ADMITTEDLY AFRAID OF COMMITMENT

but trying to get over it. Generous, affectionate, sensual, caring, 36 years old, tall, seeks woman to convert him to happily married man. You: sensual, affectionate, health-conscious, good sense of humor. Sing to me in bed.

 Men Seeking Men

I HAVE NEVER KISSED

or hugged, or made out. I am 5'10", 155 lbs., and 33 years old. You are any height, any weight, and any legal age.

 Men Seeking Women

BLAH! BLAH! BLAH!

DWM, virile 55, tall, fit, successful Blah, Blah, Blah; seeking appealing romantic, Blah, Blah, Blah, who believes CHEMISTRY IS EVERY-THING! Let's meet for some playful research.

 Women Seeking Men

WANT BIG MAN

I want a man (35-55 yrs.) with a BIG heart, BIG hands, BIG feet, who gives BIG hugs, and is ready to enjoy BIG aspects of a playful woman.

 Men Seeking Women

MR. PERFECT (NOT)

Anal-retentive DWM seeks WF who can live with broad range of idio-syncrasies that include being a Nintendomaniac, sportsaholic, and sitting on the Throne each night precisely at 10:30 p.m. to catch-up on daily reading. Of course, perfectionism dictates that you be a 10. Please reply in your neatest handwriting on plain white paper in plain white envelope.

TIRED OF THE GAME

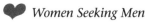 *Women Seeking Men*

BEAUTY & THE BEASTS

I'm a BEAUTY, tired of the BEASTS I've met lately!
Do handsome men exist that aren't complete trolls!?

21

TIRED OF WATCHING ROOMMATE'S HAIR FALL OUT

Desperate lonely loser, SWM, 32, miserable, apathetic, tired of watching TV and my roommate's hair fall out. Seeks depressed, unattractive SWF, 25-32, no sense of humor, for long talks about the macabre.

 Women Seeking Men

DOCTOR, LAWYER, INDIAN CHIEF

The mystery is...why is it so difficult to find a 50-something Jewish man who is intelligent, witty, stable and attractive who knows who he is and enjoys the good life? If you exist, there's one beautiful classic brunette Gemini who has been longing for you.

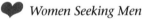 *Women Seeking Men*

GASP AT THE THOUGHT OF MARRIAGE?

If you're a man who doesn't gasp for air with the thought of marriage, and would like to have a loving relationship with a pretty, Christian, self-assured, 31, entrepreneur, write me!

 Women Seeking Men

OK, THAT'S IT

I've had it! Never liked bars much anyway. But I'm not sure about this ad stuff. Would someone convince me this is how to meet good people? DWF, 40, 5'4", full-figured, brown hair/eyes, nice smile, easygoing, down-to-earth, quiet, but witty. Good looking enough to be smooched on, admired, respected and loved to bits! If you're smiling, you may be the one!

 Women Seeking Men

I'M SICK OF GUYS WITH NO BRAINS

whose objective is to have lousy sex. Oh, God, give me a tallish man, one who weighs more than I do, and who lives his life as if he were an intelligent human being in his 30s!

Men Seeking Women

MY FRIENDS ARE MAKING ME DO THIS

I hate doing this! I'm only doing this to get them off my case! They say I have too much to offer and need to start thinking of me for a change. Hard to do with custody of two teens! Alright, already! Here goes: DWM, 46, looks 36 — feels 26. ISO attractive, intelligent, conversational non-smoker, 30-40ish. Someone who will appreciate me for who I am, not what I have; because the "ex" took all I had! There, are you guys happy now?

 Men Seeking Women

I HATE COUPLES

I am so sick of hanging out with my friends and their "other halves." Third-wheel life is a waste. If you're out there, call. SWM, 25, seeks a seeker.

 Women Seeking Men

PROVE ME WRONG!

Men feel sex is 95% of a relationship. Older men only want sweet young things. Men want women who are attractive, in good shape, yet don't take care of themselves. Are you 58-65? Any challenges?

Women Seeking Men

STOP THE ROLLER COASTER!

While cruising the midway I found all the freak shows: jobless, bankrupt, non-citizens, debtors. Reassure this classy, well-traveled, active in sports (not games) 5', 115-lb. Kewpie doll there are gentlemen 42-52 who hold the brass ring. Serious relationships only because we only go around once.

Women Seeking Men

TIRED OF WRITING ADS

I've written classy ads, sassy ads, plain ads, fancy ads, dumb ads, and funny ads. Still haven't found my soulmate. He's out there somewhere. Hints: he's a middle-aged, intelligent, nature-loving, affectionate, spiritual, outdoorsy, communicative guy with earthbound values, sense of humor, and a peaceful, kind soul. He understands a passionate life, would rather walk than ride, and prefers a sunset over TV. He's in search of an enduring, bonded LTR and looking for me!

WATCHING LOVERS IS DIFFICULT

There they go — in blue jeans, hand in each other's back pockets, taking a short cut across the field. (It is only a little longer that way.) You notice they don't speak. (There is no need to.) Each is familiar with the intoxication of talk and the difficult art of listening. And they begin to dance (waltz actually, to a very old tune only they can hear). The present they live in is Eden to them. "…Are you seeking what money can't buy?" Do you really believe the line "…till death do you part"? Would you like life to be more interesting? More than just survival? SWC boy seeking SWC girl, non-smoker. I'm 40; you should be that or less.

 Women Seeking Men

EVERYBODY'S BUDDY

Nobody's lover — just tired of being alone, and traveling alone. I'm 40+, 5'6", not slim, not boring, not ugly, very active, very personable and caring. Seek man of like qualities who is willing to "work" at building and keeping a relationship. Must like fish, horses, and me.

DROPPED ON MY HEAD

If it takes a three legged elephant, with one tusk, 5 days to cross the Sahara Desert, how many times do I have to put an ad in to get one call?

 Women Seeking Men

I'M TIRED OF MEN WHO

look for tall slinky blondes 20 years younger than they are. If you are really looking for a woman who is intelligent, attractive, confident and career-minded, then I may be for you. I need a man who is 40-55, loves romance, honest and sincere. Give me a call.

 Men Seeking Women

NO HEALTH-CONSCIOUS WOMAN FOR ME!

SWM, 58 yrs. old. I smoke, I drink… and yes, I even eat. In spite of these HORRID habits I've managed to become a successful architect. I'm looking for just one intelligent lady that is not hung up on living to be 200 years old.

GOD'S GIFT TO WOMEN

 *Men Seeking Women*

EX-SWIMWEAR MODEL

SWM, a young 33, successful professional, commitment-minded, very handsome, Mediterranean with Kennedy hair, Chippendale body, ISO a fetching, dark-haired female who's slim to medium, buxom, and enjoys being appreciated. Take a chance on this one, you won't be sorry.

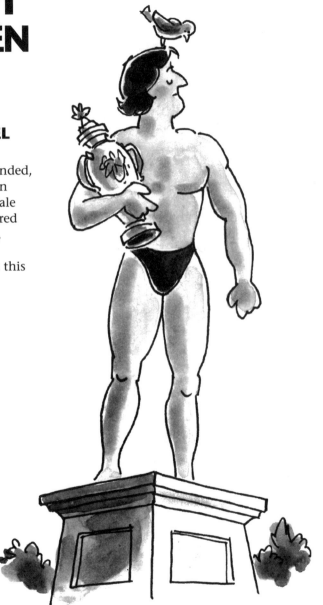

Men Seeking Women

NOT HERE TO BRAG, BUT...

I'm 21, not here to brag, but you won't find a better man in this paper. Too much to list, call for more info.

 Men Seeking Women

FORMER IVY LEAGUE PROFESSOR

Tall, attractive, PhD., 38, former Ivy League professor, now CEO of $400-million investment bank, seeks very smart, very witty, very kind, very attractive, very real person of the female variety, 25-33. On a good day, I'm funny, kind, powerful, sensitive, and able to recognize the special in the ordinary. I am incapable of catching a football or fixing a toaster, and am not very good at getting up in the morning. Please send letter with photo and phone.

 Men Seeking Women

FABIO LOOK-ALIKE

He-man type very wealthy. Body builder. Owner of several exotic cars and Caribbean islands. Seeking gal to spend my money with me. I'm gorgeous yet sensitive.

 Men Seeking Women

PHOTO EXCHANGE FIRST

Blond, blue-eyed, 6'3", 190 lbs., 30s, athletic. Print fashion model, CEO, world traveler. Seeks intensely beautiful, warmhearted, scintillating, curvaceous, family-oriented goddess, 22-30. Ready to spoil non-materialistic girl. Must be willing to lie about how we met. Photo exchange first.

 Men Seeking Women

INTERVIEWING CANDIDATES

Successful entrepreneur. Described by many a friend (and foe alike) as a World-Class Renaissance Man. Interviewing for tall, slender, blue-eyed "life stylist"/ Renaissance Woman, 20-30, for tennis, wind surfing, downhill and waterskiing, yachting, trout fishing, scuba diving, horse racing, travel, gourmet cooking and dining, music, the arts, and occasional politics. For an interview opportunity at my headquarters, you're welcome to send bio/photo/address/phone. Non-smokers. No dependents, except dogs, cats and nonvenomous animals.

 *Men Seeking Women*

LIKE NO MAN YOU'VE EVER MET

Strong, brains, kind, open, educated, fit, a success, 5'10", 172, 40, knockout looks. His new woman is 20s-30s, slim, bright, sense of humor, fit, wears heels with shorts, sweats or finest formal. Photo please.

 *Men Seeking Women*

PREFER ROYALTY OR OLD FAMILY BLOODLINES

I am a World Class man seeking a World Class woman for a long-term relationship. I am a 36-yr.-old affluent, attractive WM, who enjoys computers, travel, "the good life." I am easy to get along with, but very selective about the type of woman I wish to have in my life, one who believes as I do, that only the best will do. I prefer royalty or at least old family bloodlines. If you are overweight, a drunk, a druggy or not attractive, please do not reply. If you match my description, then please do. I ask a lot, but have a lot to give, and can search for a long time. Send for my biography.

 *Men Seeking Women*

I SHARE MY FEELINGS

Aside from the fact that I'm nice looking, successful, funny, intelligent and modest, I cook, dance, love romantic evenings (and romantic mornings), sing oldies, share feelings, enjoy sentimental movies, can make you laugh, feel wonderful and in good hands, do the food shopping and will never abuse you. I love spoiling those close to me. (I know I sound too good to be true but what if this is all true and we never meet?) I'm a youthful 49, NS/SD, tall and trim and prefer a commitment-oriented trim lady, 30s-40s, who loves lots of romance, who can appreciate me and finds mutual chemistry. NOW, what can you do for me? Let me know!

 *Men Seeking Women*

ALMOST PERFECT

Nothing is perfect in life, but I come close to it! I have looks, education, smarts, energy. I am normal, non-smoking male, and want you to be my girlfriend. I am a hard-to-find guy and won't last long, call now!

Men Seeking Women

AM I REALLY THIS GREAT?

WM, 61 yrs., 5'10", 160 lbs. Dynamic, creative, intelligent, sensitive, generous, spiritual, humorous, energetic, affectionate, and thoughtful. WOW! Am I really that great? Call or write to see for yourself. Seek a physically fit, mentally alert, spiritually aware Evangelical Christian lady who can keep up with my fast-paced, exciting life. A good body is nice; a good mind is vital.

 Men Seeking Women

CONFEDERATE REBEL

Bold Cavalier with sizable sword seeks Southern belle.

 Men Seeking Women

UNSURPASSED LOOKS!

Gorgeous male attorney/nutritionist, 31, honorable, uncommonly unpretentious, honest, virtuous, caring; nice, sincere, real, intelligent, adventurous, fun, humorous, passionate, yet with sexy, fantastic, fabulous, supreme, superb, unsur-passed looks! Seeking sincere female. Very ticklish feet absolutely crucial! LETTERS WITH PICTURES ONLY!

 *Men Seeking Women*

I DON'T WATCH FOOTBALL AND I RINSE THE SINK AFTER SHAVING

This single white male is someone quite apart from the present-day unwashed mass of male humanity. I'm 41, 6', 180 lbs., attractive, fun, sentimental, romantic, and a truly great communicator. I have real hair, don't watch football, always lower the seat and even rinse the sink after shaving. I like fine dining, I'm financially secure and have no dependents. Let's discover what we have in common!

 *Men Seeking Women*

A REAL HEAD TURNER

Used to model for Macy's to get through college, now I'm an engineer, educated, affluent, 30, tall, strikingly attractive, a real head turner, firm body, very in-shape, fun, outgoing, genuinely romantic, and a true gentleman who is searching for a pleasant, cultured, thin, and very attractive lady for exciting evenings.

KNIGHTS IN SHINING ARMOR

 *Men Seeking Women*

LANCELOT LIVES

Dashing Germanic knight with 34 yrs. of high achievement, seeks "princess" of hearts to pledge eternal love. Let's slay the dragon of mediocrity and live the Camelot experience. Only a princess with beauty and noble character will do, for this prince is everything you have dreamed of.

Men Seeking Women

TRUTH SAYER, DRAGON SLAYER, PEACEMAKER

Svelte knight and small prince banished from their kingdom, establishing new realm. Knight stands 19 hands tall and carries 11 stone, and is 1 score, 18 years. Young son 28 new moons. Seeks: damsel, daughter, comrade, co-worker, mother, lover, in order and in spirit same. There's a castle to be built, a garden to be tilled, animals to be raised and children to be taught.

 Women Seeking Men

RESCUE ME FROM DRAGON OF LONELINESS

Widowed Asian, petite 51, sexy legs, trim body, loves classical music, theater and art, needs knight in shining armor to rescue her from dragon of loneliness.

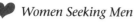 *Women Seeking Men*

DAZZLING DAMSEL

Dazzling damsel seeks tall, cerebral, 50s knight able to get his horse up to my 14th-floor apartment.

 Women Seeking Men

UNRAVISHED BRIDE OF PERSONAL ADS

Slightly sarcastic damsel seeks knight with shining imagination to rescue her from the tyranny of time. She: still unravished bride of personal ads. He: amused, tall guy paying for dinner.

 Women Seeking Men

BLACK PRINCESS

5'9", classy, beauty seeks knight to sweep her off her feet. His armor should be tall and fit enough to carry me. There is no room for baggage on our white horse. He's great in casual and formal settings. Save me before the sun sets.

 *Women Seeking Men*

RESCUE NUBIAN MAIDEN

Black knight in armor needs to rescue this Nubian maiden who hast one child. Thou may be a commoner or prince (no frogs). A gentleman who enjoys strolling, dancing, good music, and fine food washed down with wine. Break the spell. Rescue me!

BIBLE-THUMPERS

❤ *Men Seeking Women*

MINISTER SEEKS HIS PRINCESS

Spirit-filled pastor, street preacher, singing
minister seeks his princess, a woman of
God who loves street preaching and
battles for Jesus against all odds.
Make my parsonage a home. I'm
holding You in my heart, come
and let me hold You in my arms.

Women Seeking Men

NOT GOOD FOR MAN TO BE ALONE

33 yrs., 5'4", 100 lbs., brown-eyed widow with waist-length black hair and nice figure. Born-again Christian who likes cooking, gardening, and keeping a beautifully decorated home. I am loving, caring, affectionate, healthy, positive, and creative. Seek a good man, 35-50. The Lord God said, "It is not good for the man to be alone. I will make a companion suitable for him." Genesis 2:18.

 Men Seeking Women

HAS ANYONE SEEN THE GIRL I'M PRAYING ABOUT?

I'm asking Jesus for a very short, cute, never-married, long-haired, buxom girl who loves Jesus — for marriage and to have children together; a woman who believes in Biblical submission and wants to be a stay-at-home mom! I'm 37, never married, my denomination is Lutheran, but the most important thing about me is I love Jesus and He loves me!!

 *Men Seeking Women*

CONSERVATIVE BAPTIST TEACHER

SWM, 35 yrs., 5'9", 180 lbs., non-smoker, non-drinker, conservative Baptist teacher. Church participation takes precedence over all other things. I'm reserved and responsible, but caring, affectionate, and considerate. Like bowling, pets, spectator sports, dining out and quiet times at home with my special Christian lady who also loves the Lord and has a touch of the old-fashioned virtues and traits. Seek long-term or marriage.

 *Men Seeking Women*

SEEK PROVERBS 31 SWCF

Born-again SWCM, 37 yrs., 6'2", 220 lbs., sensitive, strong, but gentle. Seek Proverbs 31 SWCF, born-again, 26-40 yrs., for spiritual warfare, dining out, feeding 5,000, movies, studying lifestyles of the faithful to ultimately become one flesh and enjoy eternity forever and the new Jerusalem.

 *Men Seeking Women*

MOST IMPORTANTLY, I OBEY JESUS

I must always try my hardest to obey Jesus, Holy Spirit and God. Matt. 15:1-20, Matt. 122:22-37; WM, 34, 154 lbs., 6'2", childless, never married. Hobbies: music, volunteering. Prefer never married, childless, open communication and non-codependent. Acquaintance, friend, more?

 Men Seeking Women

THE MAN YOUR MOTHER WARNED YOU ABOUT

Into drugs (always caffeine, never nicotine), game playing (ping pong), chasing women (Christian only), church (ladies will not sit with me — I talk too much during service), walking, talking, humor, sunsets, travel, ham radio. I'm 58 yrs., 5'8", 160 lbs. Seek creative, energetic, deep faith, high values, affectionate, best friend/playmate.

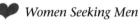 *Women Seeking Men*

GLORY HALLELUJAH!

Lonely Christian Woman has not sung Glory Hallelujah in a long time! Write Soon!

Men Seeking Women

I'LL PUT YOU IN THE TROPHY CASE OF LOVE

SWM, 43 yrs., 5'5", 150 lbs., non-smoker, and non-drinker. I've been saved for over sixteen years. I'm a "Dear" hunter and when I find her I'll put her in that trophy case of love and we'll serve the Lord together till he raptures us home. She will be a Proverbs 31 lady, WWF/SWF, 25-40, with a great sense of humor. A love of baseball/softball and cats, strongly preferred. Also country girls and nurses encouraged to reply. All replies answered. Thanks very kindly.

Men Seeking Women

CHRISTIAN VIRGINS TAKE NOTE

Single, white Bridegroom, non-smoker, drug free, 38, 6', 160 lbs. Seeks attractive, height/weight proportionate, 29- to 39-year-old single white virgin (have no carnal knowledge of any other). Photo and phone (or father's phone).

Women Seeking Men

BIBLE IN ONE HAND, HAMMER IN THE OTHER

Where is that man who is happy with a Bible in one hand and a hammer in the other? Attractive DWCF, professional, 50 yrs., 5'9", 225 lbs. Enjoy gardening, outdoors, church activities, Christian music. Seek Christian gentleman who is honest, caring, spiritually secure.

 Men Seeking Women

JOSEPH SMITH DESCENDANT

SWM, 30, independent fundamentalist Mormon. Prophet's great-great-great-grandson seeks happy, playful, loving, open-minded, spirit-filled, SWF, independent fundamentalist Mormon to age 30. Goal: Highest celestial glory. Hurry! Christ's coming.

 *Women Seeking Men*

JESUS WAS LOOKING FOR TWELVE GOOD MEN

I'm looking for one. I'm a Rubenesque SBF, 35, no kids. I'm 5'4", easygoing and enjoy movies, music and traveling. I'm seeking a kindhearted, classy Christian SM 32-45. Call me!

 *Men Seeking Women*

HE WHO FINDS A WIFE FINDETH A GOOD THING

You're out there and I know it. The thought of hearing from you is exciting. I've made the first step, now you make the next. Let's write and pray. BM, blue collar, 44 yrs., 5'8", 165 lbs. Love children.

Women Seeking Men

BIBLE AS MANUAL

Educated Christian, 45 yrs., 5'5", size 12, dark/brown, romantic, right-brained artist/writer. Seek left-brained guy who'll tolerate intuition, literature, dry humor, Bible as manual.

Men Seeking Women

GOD PROMISED

SWM, 34, 5'10", 195 lbs., non-smoker, non-drinker. My life revolves around God for love and Jesus for salvation. I need a woman to enjoy life with me, as God promised. You could be any height, but in good shape, active but guided in direction.

RURAL ROUTE ROMANCES

💜 *Men Seeking Women*

TRACTOR REPAIR A PLUS

DWM 44, 6', 175 lbs. Old-fashioned, romantic. Enjoys fishing, hunting, dining, ocean, mountains, travel. Seek old-fashioned girl who enjoys country life. Height/weight proportionate. Comfortable in silk or jeans. Knowledge of tractor repair a plus. For serious, long-term monogamous relationship and marriage. Kids welcome.

RODEOS, RANCHIN', ROPIN' & ROMANCIN'

Cowboys, Hats, Wrangler Jeans, Chaps & Spurs — they make me scream. Rodeos, Ranchin', Ropin' & Romancin', BBQ's & Brandin' & Moonlight Dancin', Saturday nights & ice cold beer, throwin' horse shoes & wranglin' steers, Cowboy ballads, Broncs & Bulls, NFR & the Western Stock Show. Qualifiers need be: Tougher than the rest, lookin' better than the best, & smoke-less. All-round amorous, financially secure. Must love life, 30 to 50. Me: One of a kind SWF, Cute, 5'4", 100 lbs., Blonde/Blue, 36, with fire in her heart & passion in her eyes. Looking for love & a Cowboy by her side. For entry form: send photo/ letter. I will reply.

 Women Seeking Men

CHIC CHICANA

seeking Chicano, age 30-45 with cowboy boots to country-western dance with a non-smokin', non-drinkin', 36-year-ol' sweet, small, shy, slender, smilin' Senorita.

 Women Seeking Men

GOOD BUTT HELPFUL

Old cowboys never die. They just ride off into the sunset! If you're 60ish WHOA! My mom is looking for you! She is shapely, in shape, looks great in jeans and on the back of her steed. Call me — her daughter — so I can inspect you. Good rider extra points. Good butt helpful.

 *Men Seeking Women*

LIVESTOCK FARMER NEEDS SPOUSE FOR THE HOUSE

SWM, 36, 5'3", 160 lbs., blue eyes, blond hair. This intelligent, hardworking young grain and livestock farmer has tractors for his fields and livestock for his barns, but doesn't have a spouse for his house. He is looking for a Christian gal, not too tall, not too wide, doesn't smoke, but is an occasional drinker and about 33-40. He enjoys picnics and BBQs, bowling and fishing, movies and volleyball, anything simple and relaxing.

Women Seeking Men

OLD CHEVY TRUCKS

WF, 44 yrs., likes chickens, rain, 18-wheelers, gardens, staying home, old Chevy trucks…and you?

 Men Seeking Women

I CAN COOK, CLEAN, AND MAKE A LADY SCREAM

DW Country Boy, 43, 5'10", 165 lbs., short dark hair, and bright blue eyes. I'm told I'm handsome and have a perfect life, but what I lack is a pretty country wife. I can cook, I can clean, and make a lady scream, but what I need is a woman to grow old with to fulfill all my dreams.

 Men Seeking Women

UGLIER THAN A BUCKET OF RATTLESNAKES

DWM, 45 yrs., and uglier than a bucket of rattlesnakes. I chew tobacco and am bowlegged, but I take my hat off at the dinner table. If you can bake an apple pie and kiss this ugly face, then I want to hear from you.

 *Women Seeking Men*

LISTEN UP, ALL YOU COWBOYS

Are you 5'10" or taller, 30-50, searching for someone to make you smile, laugh, help take life's load off your shoulders, put up the fence, take care of the animals? Well, this attractive, young 42, 5'8", 130 lbs., long blonde, blue eyes, horse massage therapist, pet groomer would like to help. Rodeos, animals, sunsets, hugs, romance, hard worker. Warm and sensitive, sense of humor, and willing to relocate.

 Men Seeking Women

I'M NO CASANOVA

but I swear this much is true: I'll be holding nothing back when it comes to you. I will give you my heart, be all that you need. DWM, 31, 6', 200 lbs., brown/brown. Full-time dad to a cute little cowgirl of six. I'm seeking a slim country girl, 25-35. Into romance, roses, life, love, and laughter. I'm not into games. I'm looking for that special lady to give me that butterflies-in-the-stomach feeling. Is this you? I hope so.

Women Seeking Men

TALL WITH A MUSTACHE?

Wanted: A man 38-49 who rises early, likes a tidy home, loves watching children play and appreciates the tales of old men. Honesty and a sharing nature a must. Should like the outdoors, horses, and all that goes with it. If you like cowboy poetry, riding the range, and are tall, with a mustache, that would be a plus!

 Men Seeking Women

I CLEAN UP NICE

If you are a SWF, physically attractive, trim, 29-39, don't smoke (or chew), and know enough about horses to realize that a fetlock is not a form of bondage, I'd like to tell you about myself. I'm secure and stable (no pun intended), a 5'11", 195 lbs. non-smoker, SWM, divorced with no children. I don't appeal to everyone, but my friends (not just my Mom) think I "clean up nice" and that I have an excellent sense of humor. I'm seeking someone to share my varied interests, including country dancing, scuba diving, and a rural lifestyle built around my suburban hobby farm, horses and trail riding. You need not be an excellent horseperson, but you must share a love for nature and horses.

 *Men Seeking Women*

I LIKE
HONEST HORSES
AND HONEST FRIENDS

DW Cowboy, 6'2", 235 lbs., 42 yrs., handsome, rugged. Sometimes bearded, always moustachioed. Bit and spurmaker, silversmith, occasional poet, fun-loving and hard-working. I like honest horses, honest friends, Blueheeler pups, open spaces, hunting, waltzes, and thunderstorms. Looking for romantic reality with SW lady, tall (5'10"+), attractive, healthy, 30-40 yrs., weight proportionate. Must be honest, open, caring, and a friend. Must understand a cowboy's life of early mornings, black coffee, haying, fixing fence, branding, checking cows, cowboy poetry, spade bits, riatas, and old Navajo rugs.

Men Seeking Women

HOMEGROWN, CORN-FED
FARM GIRL WANTED

by SM, 32 yrs., for friendship and maybe marriage. Must be very funny, playful, nice, with a cool wit and a well-developed sense of humor. Hourglass shape, live anywhere in the U.S.

ODDBALLS

❤ *Men Seeking Women*

SEND PHOTO OF HUNTING DOGS

You love anything outdoors and hunting (especially deer, boar, and turkey), movies, music, dining, travel (I have a lifetime pass), gardening, sports you play. ME: DWM, tall, non-smoker, non-drinker, no drugs. Easy-going, approaching middle age with original hair & teeth. Have "Grizzly Adams" looks and "Columbo" ways. Union job, country home and I'm a good cook. P.S. — If you have hunting dogs, send photo of them.

Women Seeking Men

WELCOME TO THE TWILIGHT ZONE

where the mundane isn't permitted! Writer, poet, songwriter, open-minded, creative, agnostic, non-smoker. Loves nature, animals, UFO investigation, parapsychology/metaphysics.

 Men Seeking Women

EVEN PUT SEAT DOWN!

But she still left me! Like, being Mr. Manners has its downside. I put the seat down when my girlfriend visited. What did it get me? Heartache?! She said she didn't like the seat down, she started screaming, and left me for a guy who left his seat UP! She was just a bit strange. Seems I attract gorgeous women who lack common sense. I even do windows, and my other girlfriend says she didn't even do HOUSE! Guess who cleaned the toilet? Yep. Story of my life, no respect. Beautiful, sweet ladies, yet none that match my mind and wit. Hope you smiled. I am 30ish, gentle, upbeat, firm body, 5'10", 167 lbs., athletic and self-employed.

 *Women Seeking Men*

CUTE GUY WITH SNOWPLOW

sought by head-turnin', zany, brainy, late 30s Babe to share happy times in the big driveway of love. A rake for spring a big plus!

 Women Seeking Men

I'M A NUT

Adventurous like a macadamia, sweet as a praline, and a smile like a butternut. I pick out the good ones that I enjoy. You: A primo cashew, slightly coconuts, and definitely not a goober or filbert. You're 30-40, straightforward, educated, caring, into arts, music, and concerts.

 *Women Seeking Women*

LIPSTICK LESBIAN FLAME

45, the eternal type, seeks match who sensitively and successfully focuses her own light. No moths, please.

Men Seeking Women

SPRING CABIN FEVER

and some parts have been cooped up longer than others. And the church single groups haven't come through and my bowling game is suffering and no more bars. But other than that, we're perfect for each other. I'm 6'3", 47, and 170, and I hope you're not.

 Women Seeking Men

RUNNING ON EMPTY...

I like driving around with my two cats, especially on the freeway. I make them wear little hats so that I can use the carpool lane. Way too much time on your hands too? Call me. SWF, 42, 5'10", brown/blue.

 Women Seeking Women

TEACH ME
HOW TO COOK
VEGGIE MEALS

GWF, 36, brown hair, green eyes, veggie. Into: bodybuilding, lesbian avengers, dyke marches, herbs, and pretty, mature, monogamous "femmes." Teach me how to cook veggie meals. I order out all the time. Looking for that "special for me" lover. HIV+ welcome.

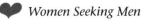 *Women Seeking Men*

SEEK GULLIBLE MALE

Coldhearted, insensitive, unconscionable, selfish, hedonistic, drunk liar seeks next gullible male without enough sense to stay away from me.

 Women Seeking Men

PUBLIC SERVICE
MESSAGE

Studies prove that professional men, age 50s, who are unattached, risk more health problems than others. But if you're a man of warmth, wit and intellect, you could escape this dangerous lifestyle by meeting an accomplished, sophisticated woman who is trim, fit and shapely (5'7"), with a lovely, healing smile.

 Men Seeking Women

MENTALLY ILL?

Are you restrained in a straight-jacket? Do you think you're a chicken? Did you kill and eat your last boyfriend? I don't mind. This tall, educated, professional SWM would like to meet an interesting woman!

Men Seeking Women

NOT NORMAL

Tall, dark, handsome SWM, late 30s, darkly humorous, highly intelligent, noncorporate, old soul/young heart, financially/emotionally secure, interests include: organic forms, platonic ideals, comfortable shoes, frivolous digressions, exotic condiments. Seeking tall, dark, attractive, intelligent, funny, independent, creative woman, who dreams of a simple life with a good man.

 Women Seeking Men

MY CLOSET:

Riding boots, velvet, silk, heels, skis, racquet, mitt, soccer ball, jazz, passport, ribbons for long red hair. Master Fine Arts, 41, 5'6", dark eyes, decent build seeking upbeat big guy, arts streak, degreed. Let's get younger together.

 Men Seeking Women

I'M NOT

married, divorced or in the clergy. Not bald. Not a Democrat. Not rich. Not starving. Not into C&W. Not afforded traditional hours due to working in restaurant management. Not over 33. Not under 6'2". Not over 190 lbs. Not into being single anymore. Not a bad guy.

 Men Seeking Women

INTERESTING FLAWS

I'm a SWM, 6', 175 lbs., 38. I'm told I'm attractive. I like to laugh, but I know what's funny and what isn't. I own a great old house and live with a big white dog and two kittens. I am a professional. Children are important to me. Someday with the right person I would like a family. You can lie about your age some, but please be in your early to mid-thirties. Be free (no hang-ups for ex's). Like your work. Don't lie about your weight please; one woman called and gained over 60 lbs. between the time we talked on the phone and the time I met her the next day. I have only a couple of absolutes; no drugs at all, and no excessive drinking or smoking. Other than that, I would prefer it if you had some interesting flaws. Perfection isn't very attractive.

 Men Seeking Women

SOCIAL MISFIT

Seeking caffeine-buzzed, spontaneous social misfit willing to take unreasonable risk in love and life before the other shoe drops.

Women Seeking Men

CASABLANCA

She walked into the party in her tight-fitting black jeans that showed every curve of her slender 5'10" body. She radiated beauty and confidence. She pushed her long blonde hair over her shoulder, then their eyes met. He was tall, dark and handsome. He must have been in his 40s. He was rugged, and yet professional looking. As he began to walk across the room, he took a drag of his cigarette and a sip of his coffee. Is this you?

 Men Seeking Women

HAIR DARE

Seeking gutsy, daring woman with long, thick hair, willing to get a crewcut even closer than mine. Bold adventuress who meets dare gets long-term commitment from attractive, successful, single, white professional male. There must be a confident spirit out there who can't pass up the dare. Call!!

 Men Seeking Women

TELEPHONE RELATIONSHIP

SM, 32 yrs., looking for a phone relationship only. Call me.

Women Seeking Men

LEGGY BLONDE BIMBO

posing as professional career girl seeks someone special — preferably someone who can wash own socks and burn own toast. Be different — call me.

Men Seeking Women

NO DATE IN 140 MONTHS

34-year-old widower with 4-year-old son. I drink, play pool, and love alternative rock music. I'm smart (can speak Chinese) and handsome. Did I mention the pierced tongue? 5'11", height/weight proportionate.

Women Seeking Men

WANT MERCEDES MECHANIC

Wanted: the Mercedes Mechanic of my dreams. Creative, elegant, scatterbrained, and balanced female: music lover, classically trained chef, former catfish farmer, engineering techie seeks diesel kinda guy for '77 renovation.

Men Seeking Women

CALENDAR GIRL WANTED

If you're cute like a bunny and romantic like Cupid, then spring forward, don't fall back. Hop on my lap and tell this 5'9", 165 lb., 40-year-old Santa what you really desire. No witches or turkeys, please.

 Men Seeking Women

I AM HOMELESS

My age is 37, my height is 5'8", my weight is 185. I can't reed or rite. I have no car or house. I'm kind of homeless and feel like people are following me. I got black and white tv, Wapner comes on at 4 o'clock, I smell good sometimes on fridays, and I like women who shave. Sorry, what you have read is totally bogus. I have an outrageous, funny personality. Let's get in touch and you can hear the real story.

 *Men Seeking Women*

I AMS WHAT I AM

Popeye seeks Olive Oyl. I ams what I am, SWPM, with a Bluto appetite for sharing a can of spinach with my long lost lady, Olive Oyl. Extra virgin unimportant. Wimpys need not apply. Auk … auk … auk … auk.

 *Women Seeking Men*

MY NECK IS ALL YOURS

SWF, 27, obnoxious, silly, pierced, tattooed, insane, hormonally unbalanced, roller-blading, sushi-eating, cartoon-watching redhead from Hell, seeks Vlad. My neck is all yours. BITE ME.

 *Women Seeking Men*

GLUTTON FOR PUNISHMENT

Invisible, golden-hearted spirit, seeks slovenly, crazed yet cerebral tyrant to help take the edge off the grind. Tolerance for kindness a plus. Please be unattractive, unsuccessful, and anti-eclectic.

 *Men Seeking Women*

HEARTBREAKER WANTED

Award-winning poet, 27 yrs., seeks short-term, intense, doomed relationship for inspiration. Must be attractive, sensual, articulate, ruthless, 21-30 yrs., under 5'6". Break my heart, please.

HUBBA! HUBBA!

 *Men Seeking Women*

PARTIAL COUCH POTATO

SBM, 32, heavy-set, shy, but intelligent, loveable and funny. Likes Scrabble, talk radio and books. ISO childless, full-figured SF, for reading, watching cable and eating.

Women Seeking Men

LIFE IN THE FAT LANE

It's slow, self-indulgent and comfy but sometimes it's lonely. Would you like to walk this path with me? Interesting, large WF, 40s, seeks a non-smoking, interesting boyfriend.

 Women Seeking Men

DO YOU GET COLD IN THE WINTER?

I've got the solution: 420 lbs. of ice-melting curves. So let's break the ice. Successful SWF, Christian, 32, educated professional who enjoys conversation, traveling and sharing snowcones.

 Men Seeking Women

WHAT'S YOUR BRA SIZE?

Mediterranean hunk, incredibly attractive, body builder, 37, seeking Hispanic or white females, 18-30 who wear super-customized bras.

 *Men Seeking Women*

CHUBBY CHERUB

Cute, chubby cherub, SWM, 50, 5'8", ISO special friend and lover with really dirty mind to live and laugh and love happily ever after.

 *Men Seeking Women*

BOTTOM-HEAVY ONLY

SWM, 28, handsome, military, 6', 210 lbs., ISO beautiful perfect pear-shaped, bottom-heavy 4-real woman. I am marriage-minded, honest, clean, passionate, and almost perfect.

 *Men Seeking Women*

AMAZON WANTED

for sexy fun. Be: 250-400 lbs.; 5'7" to 6'4"; very broad shoulders, even wider hips, giant anaconda thighs and big bear-hugging arms. Age/race open. Liking for travel a plus. DWM, professional, 48, 5'8", slim, youthful, physically fit, sensuous; overseas but returning soon. Your full-length photo/ phone number gets mine. Beat me at arm wrestling and I am yours forever!

Women Seeking Men

BIG FAT MAMA

I'm unreliable, undisciplined, irresponsible, inefficient, immature, but I'm fun. Seeking SWM, 38-50, to have fun with and cuddle. If you'd like some well-padded, wide-body luxury, give me a call.

 Men Seeking Women

CHIC OF ARABY

I'm actually Jewish. Investor, 36, seeks to wed fertile, un-divorced, VERY pearshaped "belly dancer." Jewish/ethnic, supersize preferred.

 Men Seeking Women

SEEK BUBBLE BUTT

Handsome DWM, 40, blonde/blue, muscular, 5'8", 180 lbs., seeks loving, gentle, romantic S/DWF with round, bulging bubble butt and pretty face with monogamous intentions, 28-40, culture, nature, cats, romantic evenings and desire LTR with soulmate and best friend.

 Men Seeking Men

LOOKING FOR BIG DADDY

400+ lbs. for wrestling and hot times. I'm 26, 6', 255 lbs. and a first timer.

 Women Seeking Men

FAT OLDER WOMAN

SWF, 47, 5'10", 240 lbs. (I look younger, thinner, and shorter — but so what?) Woefully disorganized, casual dresser, average looks. Creative, verbal, agile brain. Desires younger (or younger-thinking) man.

 *Women Seeking Men*

SHORT, FAT, UGLY, COULD BE YOUR DREAM COME TRUE

You need a good sense of humor, have at least half a brain, and the ability to speak. Tall, dark, great looking a plus. Dancing a must. Be brave and call.

 *Women Seeking Men*

PORTLY, ROBUST, CORPULENT ...

Some women find large men sexy and attractive, as well as huggable! If you enjoy the company of smaller women, are intelligent, sincere, honest, and financially stable, and enjoy cultural events, dining out, movies, the mountains, quiet conversation, and are not into drugs or the bar scene, give me a call.

Women Seeking Men

FULL ROUNDED RUMP AND TUMMY

SWF, blonde, blue-eyed, 400+ lbs., tall, with long, soft legs, full rounded rump and tummy! ISO SWM who's warm, nice, and full of fun — you!

 Men Seeking Women

NO DIETERS PLEASE

SWM, 40, 6' tall, 210 lbs., Italian, NS, very healthy, looking for a large lady to spend some time with. I travel a lot and would like to meet for dinner or movies when I'm in your town. No dieters please. I like bringing sweets when I come calling. So don't be shy, especially the extra-extra-extra large ladies. I will answer all very politely.

 Men Seeking Women

NO WEIGHT LOSS OR CHILDREN

Romantic, affectionate, sensuous DWM, 39, 5'9", with medium but muscular build, seeks monogamous relationship with a lady whose plans are void of weight loss and children.

 Women Seeking Men

JELLY BELLY

"Lonewolf" ISO Leader of the Pack! I'm 29, 5'7", 235 lbs., sweet, thick thighs, a jelly belly too.

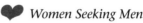 *Women Seeking Men*

LUSCIOUSLY SOFT

Pretty DWF, 40s, 300 lbs., 5'4", 56D-50-68, lusciously soft, fat arms, huge blubbery belly and back, nicely rounded bottom, intelligent, fun loving, affectionate. ISO attractive S/DWM any age, average to muscular build who thinks fat is beautiful, sensuous, and sexy, and desires friendship/romance and sharing life's pleasures.

 Men Seeking Women

CELLULITE LOVER

SWM, 6'1", 220 lbs., nice looking, cellulite lover, seeks mate with extra-wide, firm calves (over 22"), age 35-50, for long-term relationship.

THE STURGIS CROWD

 Women Seeking Men

FREEDOM FIRE BURNIN' IN MY SOUL

Five-foot-eight with eyes of gold, got a freedom fire burnin' in my soul. Want to pack behind a man of pride, who's into adventure and living life. WF, 31, sun-streaked brown hair, gold eyes, lonesome for a lover's arms at night, for eyes that connect in the day. For that song only a Harley sings. Seger says it best, "Roll, roll me away, won't you roll me away tonight. I too am lost, I feel double-crossed, and I'm sick of what's wrong and what's right." Looking for someone real, a man who loves being in the wind as much as me. Who can share rough roads with the smooth. Who is semi-crazy but mostly responsible. If that's you, please reply.

Women Seeking Men

BUGS ON YOUR TEETH?

Enjoy wind in your hair and bugs on your teeth? Come ride with 49-year-old, non-smoking, caring, attractive DWF. Prefer stocky, muscular.

 Women Seeking Men

MOTORCYCLE MAMA

Where are you? S/DWM 35-45? Let's take a ride on your Harley. I'm ready for that white collar, wild inside man. You won't be disappointed with this DWF, 45 going on 29, who knows what to do with those leathers. I'm looking for adventure, whatever comes our way.

 Men Seeking Women

NO SPACE CASES

Short WM, blue eyes, Harley rider, seeks warm-hearted lady, prefer 25-35. Must like kids and serious riding. No dopers, thieves, or space cases. Personality more important than looks or age. Ambitious to work together. Christian type okay.

 *Men Seeking Women*

A TATTOOED LADY

Companion with exotic piercing is my passion. SWM with extensive body art, requires a female counterpart. So let's get together.

 Men Seeking Women

WASH-AND-WEAR PERSONALITY

DW dad, 140 lbs., blond hair, blue eyes, beard, pierced ear, enjoys amusement park, motorcycle/car races, videos, small pubs, music, seeking SF, to spend time.

 Women Seeking Men

HIPPIES & HARLEYS

Single white female, 5'5", 120 lbs., 30, red hair, green eyes in search of a single white male with "bad" bike. I want a tall, thin biker to share wild times, must be able to take me as I am. Tattoos and body piercing a plus. Send photo. All calls answered.

USED CAR LOT

♥ *Men Seeking Women*

BACKFIRES OCCASIONALLY

1960 bachelor, white with brown top, two seater (not a family car), rips mile in 7:00, doesn't smoke (backfires occasionally), sluggish on cold mornings, 77" long, great fenders, no rust.

Women Seeking Men

BIG 1949 CADDY

Follow me. I could change your life. Vintage 1949 Cadillac, lush, plush, big and well-padded seeks experienced SWM, non-smoking driver with clear eyes and steady hands. Cat lover purrferred.

 Men Seeking Women

HANDLES CURVES WELL

Good body, low mileage, all terrain, off road; sports utility with comfortable roomy interior, smooth acceleration and cruise control. Exceptional response and handling. Smokes a little, with solid stick shift and handles curves well. No air bags; shoulder straps and sound system included. Reasonable offers only, financing available.

 Men Seeking Women

NEED A TUNE-UP?

Used 1962 WM model seeking 1958-1965 new or used female model in need of tune up. Alcohol combustible or speeders need not apply. Model must have rugged terrain where there's plenty of hiking, camping and fishing. Minor body work acceptable, no lemons!

 Women Seeking Men

GREAT SET OF WHEELS

The Black Caddy's cruising 40-50, long, sleek, great headlights, streaks past the white Jag. She's at 40-something, classy, great set of wheels. He swerves, she swerves, they spin, sparks are flying, they ignite and ?

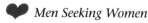 *Men Seeking Women*

I'M TOO SEXY FOR MY CAR

A Jeep Wagoneer with wood paneling. But don't be afraid. I've got AAA qualities (attractive, athletic, affectionate), 28, SWM, 5'11", my needs simple — I look for bi-pedal motion, active frontal lobes, a sense of adventure, and a creative wit. Exceptional SWF 24-30. Please reply.

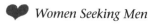 *Women Seeking Men*

TURBO MOM

Low mileage, mint condition, 1952, white, completely restored turbo mom. Seeks D/SPWM, dependable, 1946-58 classic, doesn't need work under hood. Non-smoker, non-drinker. Owner won't carry.

JAILBIRDS

 Men Seeking Women

MY FUTURE IS BRIGHT, ALL I NEED IS YOU.

Former bank robber, now in prison…still reading? SWM, 38, 6'3",
210, brown/green. Stereotype doesn't apply. I owned a popular
restaurant and lounge, lake home. No phony macho act, I'm a real
man. Communication, intimacy assured. Out soon, financially
secure, relocatable.

Men Seeking Women

WELL-OFF PRISONER WILL PROVIDE FINANCIAL ASSISTANCE

Ladies: Well-off prisoner and former engineer seeks fine, sexually outgoing and loving lady to help do his time, share two-day family visits, and make mad, passionate love. Will provide financial assistance of up to $500 per month. Ideal for single mother. I'm intelligent, good-looking, 6'1", 185 lbs., 30, and fun-loving. Write and send pictures.

 Men Seeking Women

OH, THOSE WALLS

I know there's a fine lady out there who can help me get my mind off these walls.

 Women Seeking Men

BLUE-EYED MERMAID

25-year-old, blue-eyed mermaid is about to regain her beautiful legs so that she can walk with her dream man. Age unimportant.

 *Men Seeking Women*

THE JUDGE SAID LIFE, FRIENDS SAID GOOD-BYE

The Judge said life; friends and family said good-bye. SWM, 6'1", 225 lbs. in need of someone to write to.

Women Seeking Men

WILD AND BEAUTIFUL AS AN ASIAN TIGRESS

SBF, 27. If you rub my belly just right, I'm a kitten. Wanted: older gent to find the right spots to make me purr. Incarcerated, put full name and address on envelope.

Men Seeking Women

TIGHT-FITTING GENES

My DNA must find its match! A natural selection in tight-fitting genes would be ideal. I am looking for an evolving relationship with a distinguishable primate of the female persuasion. Incarcerated.

NERDS & GEEKS

💜 *Men Seeking Women*

REVENGE OF THE NERDS

Thick glasses, HP calculator, SAT 99th percentile, knows pi to 16 digits. Great job, big house, pool. SWM, 33, 6'0", 144 lbs. Better looking than Bill Gates.

Men Seeking Women

SHY MATH GENIUS

Author/computer scientist and rock & roller with hidden ponytail and earplugs, politically liberal, happy, sincere, sensitive guy, 30+, seeks similar partner to share life's great adventure.

 Men Seeking Women

SCAN MEETS SCAN

Hi-tek female friend wanted! This incredibly wonderful guy (full of adverbs and adjectives) is looking for a lady who knows how to scan her photo (clean only) and exchange with me online. I propose this up-front and unique offer. Why? I want you to know what I look like, just as if we passed on the street. You get for your effort a WM (gets better! be patient!), charming, 30s, sense of humor (you can always spot a bachelor cuz he comes to work from different directions), looks (photo, you will receive), brains (know what I had for breakfast yesterday), professional (not a garbage man), and loves nature, animals and meeting you. Scan your photo and write me now!

 Men Seeking Women

I WANT BRAINS

"Igor, find me brains." Brains with a woman attached, 5'3"-5'9", 24-33, not large, who likes mad scientists or better yet, goofy SWM engineers.

 Women Seeking Men

RESCUE ME FROM CHAT ROOMS!

Need guy pal to distract me from mindless addiction to chat rooms. Humor and intelligence appreciated. Non-smoking preferred. Respond with twelve alternative activities we could enjoy together.

 *Men Seeking Men*

COMPUTE THYSELF

GWM, 27, 6'2", 215 lbs., seeks sane computer geek with a healthy sense of the absurd. No internet addicts, please!

MIRROR, MIRROR ON THE WALL...

 *Women Seeking Men*

TRUST ME...TRUST ME...I'M WONDERFUL

Impossible to describe in six lines of newsprint, but trust me, I'm wonderful. SWF, 34, blue eyes, and great smile, seeks sexy, intelligent WM, non-smoker, 24-42, to fall in love with.

Women Seeking Men

SEXY MOM, NOT YOUR TYPICAL GIRL NEXT DOOR

I'm a great catch and have it all — model looks, a heart of gold, and a positive attitude. I'm outgoing, optimistic, sophisticated, and down-to-earth. I'm in my late 20s, 5'5", 115 lbs., blonde hair, green eyes. Looking for someone who also has it all — looks, money, attitude, and a kind heart. The possibilities are endless and you won't be disappointed.

 Women Seeking Men

I LOVE TIGHT SWEATERS AND SHORT SKIRTS...

because I look good in them. Buxom redhead loves a good joke, has an Ultrabrite smile and a disposition to match. Seeking a doctor, lawyer, or businessman over 35, who loves movies, travel, dining and who wants to be pampered by a lady.

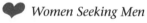 *Women Seeking Men*

BEAUTIFUL WILDFLOWER

Dazzling blue-eyed blonde, 5'4", 108 lbs., 34 (looks 24). Delicate body, perky personality, professional career. Seeking rugged tumbleweed guy with great looks, successful career, strong character and irresistible charm.

 Women Seeking Men

I GET ALL THE ATTENTION

My friends say they don't like going to parties with me because I get all the attention. Tall blonde seeks tall, good-looking, spontaneous, active male to share the fun things life has to offer.

 *Women Seeking Men*

A TRUE 9

Professional SWF, non-smoker/social drinker, 39, 5'7", 130 lbs., well built, self-confident, a true 9. Anything outdoors interests me, as does writing, singing, acting, social events, movies. If you're SWM/SHM, non-smoker/social drinker, age 30-45, a true 9, physically fit (no beer bellies), good looking (but not conceited), intelligent, a macho dude (but sensitive), let's talk.

Women Seeking Men

STUNNING STEWARDESS

seeks savvy success! 5'8", 30-something, vivacious brunette, gourmet cook, seeking career-devoted "power- type." If you're used to the best, and would like the best for love and marriage, call or write. I'll be behind you 100%.

THE SINGLES JUNGLE

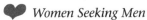 *Women Seeking Men*

MOMMY BEAR

DWF, 39, plus size with cubs and stable career. Seeks Daddy Bear, 37-47, with same to share honey pot. Who enjoys camping, fishing, hunting, country life, spending time cuddling while watching TV or time with family. Who's honest, considerate to others. Smoker, occasional drinker okay.

Women Seeking Men

LAST MATE
WAS A SQUIRREL
WHO WENT NUTS

I was hibernating but now I am hunting for a sly, large white animal with papers and resources for frolicking in the concrete forest and nuzzling in the den. Keen instincts needed to lead the chase. I will not set traps.

 Women Seeking Men

SEEKING TOMCAT

Pretty Kitty seeks Tomcat to howl and prowl with. I am a 37-yr.-old, 5'2." blonde tiger with green eyes (no kittens). I am a homeowner and a professional. Tell me why I should write you back and I will...if you don't, I won't. P.S. I love to purr and I am not declawed; bring own catnip!

 Men Seeking Women

JUNGLE BOOGIE

Attorney, 32, no time for safari, seeks beautiful, long-haired lioness for jungle boogie and romance. You: smart, fit, outgoing.

 Women Seeking Men

ON THE PROWL

Seductive, 46, 5'2", 135 lbs., she-cat on the loose with streamline curves like a jaguar waiting to pounce on her tom. She likes travel, movies, music, and sports. She has been declawed so you won't get hurt. If you are the purrfect tom, come roam the jungle with me.

 Men Seeking Women

JACKRABBIT

wants Cottontail for long winter nights. He: handsome and white, 44. She: active, attractive 30-40. Must have cute tail.

 Women Seeking Men

LUV PUPPY
WANTED

Must have a full head of fur and be loyal and faithful, preferred age 5-7 in dog years, must be a cuddler who likes to have his head and belly scratched. Tall SWM, who doesn't drool and doesn't need grooming is great.

WILD MUSTANG

Well-bred racehorse with a streak of wild mustang is tired of running alone. This 5'9", 30-year-old filly has long legs, blue eyes, and blonde mane. She's high spirited, independent but loyal. Likes open spaces, starry nights, unique watering holes, and racing with the wind.

BATMAN CALL CATWOMAN

SWF, 26, 5'10", blonde/brown, likes cats, bats and everything in between. My purrfect mate: SWM, 25-35, 4'10"+, active and adventurous, who likes dancing, hiking, pool and pouncing around at night. Don't be a joker, pick up the bat phone and tell me what's under your cape.

DOG WANTED

Snoopy type, no butts, best friend, unconditional love; take me to the park/playground. Must nurture pets, teen puppy left in doghouse. Lost: Woodstock searching for the Red Baron. Fetch mail only. Reward: a friend forever.

CAN CHEETAH COME OUT AND PLAY?

Yes, it is I! Dominant, aggressive, full-figured white woman. Can cheetah come out and play? R-R-R-R! I am physically double x, mentally triple x. I like my coffee like I like my men...hot, black, and lots of sugar! Only gentle and considerate gentlemen need reply. Manners a plus!

FRISKY AT FORTY

Pretty, green-eyed, little feline is bored with chasing her tail, sitting, watching world go by. She's looking for her special "Tom" to bring back the glow in her eyes, pounce in her prance. He'll cuddle her, love her, make her purr once again. Together they'll explore life's adventures. No "Garfields" please!

DOG OR FOX?

An ugly woman is often called a "dog," whereas a pretty woman is a "fox." If a dog is a man's best friend, why go on a fox hunt? It may turn out to be a wild-goose chase.

Men Seeking Women

A REAL DOG

Large, loyal, affectionate, trainable obedient. Works like a dog. Mixed breed, sort of St. Bernard or German Shepherd. Rarely barks. Never bites. Needs good home. Healthy, strong. Woof, woof.

 Women Seeking Men

WILD FILLY

Ready to be tamed. High spirited, playful, attractive, petite frame, 5'2" stature, auburn mane, dark green eyes. Needs mature, experienced man with slow hand, firm touch, soothing voice. You be 40ish, attractive, loving & fit for long workouts.

 Men Seeking Women

TIGRESS CAPTURES LION

Tigress, tigress burning bright, in the passion of full flight; I wish we may, I wish we might, Breathe sweet soft words together tonight. Extraordinary attorney, SWM, 40, 6', 170 lbs. (fit), seeks professional, spirited Hispanic/Black/White 25-38, untamed, clawed tigress whose unforgettable voice and smile will cage this lionhearted man.

 Men Seeking Women

THROW YOUR HOOK INTO MY POND

If you have the right bait, I might bite. What's the right bait, you ask yourself? Put this on your hook! Reasonably fit, great attitude, varied interests, 30-38 years old, adventurous, feminine, and attractive. This catch has blue/brown, white, 5'7" body with some freckles, a lot of hair, nice white teeth, and a great set of lips. I've heard I'm a trophy in my 41 years in the pond. Remember the saying, 'You can't catch anything if you don't have your hook in the water.' Be a sport. Throw the line. Photo appreciated.

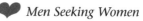 *Men Seeking Women*

SEEK CAVE MATE

Lonely Teddy Bear seeks cave mate for the coming winter. Female should be shorter than the average brown bear and not too heavy. I am frisky and seek playful she bear wanting to travel, dine out and do exciting things. Lady bears between 45-55 should reply.

KATHY HINCKLEY

Sexy DWF with green eyes, dark brown hair (most of the time), and real fingernails. Closet stuffed with three sizes of clothing to accommodate yo-yo weight. Collect personal ads and fantasy postcards, and love to have my feet rubbed. Grew up on a cattle ranch in South Dakota. Professional genealogist and lecturer. Two adult children, one teenager, and two cats.

GARY REGESTER

PETER HESSE

MWM, non-smoker, no drugs, will never see 60 again. Original hair and teeth, 6', 170 lbs. First marriage: two sons, one daughter; second marriage: one daughter. Five grandkids. Loves travel, sports, movies, good books and painting watercolors. Lifetime in advertising, graphic design and cartooning. Rhode Island native, living in Denver since 1969.

Kathy and Peter
Seek More Ads

Have you read any personal ads lately that were unusual or made you laugh? If so, we would love to receive a copy for our expanding resource file. Mail the ads to:

Plain Fat Chick
P.O. Box 40367
Denver, CO 80204-0367

E-mail: PLAINCHICK@aol.com